Inside Blender: A Tale of 3D Creation and Discovery by Alex Ishikawa.

Chapter 1: Discovering Blender - The Spark of Curiosity: Alex hears about Blender for the first time and begins to explore what makes this software a favorite among 3D artists.

Chapter 2: The Download Decision - Taking the Leap: Alex decides to download Blender, walking through the process of finding and installing the software on his computer.

Chapter 3: First Launch - Entering a New World: Alex opens Blender for the first time, experiencing the initial wonder and complexity of the interface.

Chapter 4: Navigating the Interface - Learning the Ropes: A detailed guide through Blender's interface, helping Alex understand the layout, tools, and key features.

Chapter 5: Your First Project - Creating a Simple Object: Alex starts with a basic project to get familiar with Blender's modeling tools.

Chapter 6: Sculpting and Texturing - Bringing Shapes to Life: Alex learns about sculpting and texturing in Blender, adding detail and realism to his models.

Chapter 7: Lighting and Rendering - The Art of Visualization: This chapter introduces Alex to the world of lighting and rendering, essential for bringing his 3D models to life.

Chapter 8: Animation Basics - Giving Motion to Models: Alex delves into the basics of animation in Blender, learning how to make his creations move.

Chapter 9: Exploring Advanced Features - Beyond the Basics: Alex explores more advanced features of Blender, such as particle systems, physics simulations, and more complex animation techniques.

Chapter 10: Completing Your First Project - From Start to Finish: Alex applies all he has learned to complete his first comprehensive project in Blender, culminating his journey from a beginner to a confident user.

Chapter 1: Discovering Blender - The Spark of Curiosity

In the quiet corner of a bustling college library, Alex sat hunched over his laptop, his eyes scanning through a digital art forum. He had always been fascinated by 3D art and animation, but the world of 3D modeling software seemed daunting. That was until he stumbled upon a thread raving about Blender.

The First Encounter

"Blender," he read aloud, a sense of curiosity rising within him. The forum members spoke of Blender with a passion he had rarely seen. It was free, open-source, and boasted a range of features that rivaled expensive professional software. Alex's interest was piqued. Could this be the tool to unlock his creative potential?

Unraveling the Blender Mystique

He delved deeper, watching videos and reading articles. Blender wasn't just a modeling tool; it was a complete suite for rendering, animation, sculpting, and even video editing. The versatility amazed him. He saw stunning artwork and animations, all created in Blender, and realized the power that this software held.

Overcoming the Intimidation

Yet, with every showcase of breathtaking renders and intricate models, a wave of intimidation washed over him. He wondered, "Can a beginner like me really learn this?" But amidst the forums, he found a community of Blender enthusiasts, sharing their learning journeys and encouraging newcomers. It wasn't just a software; it was a gateway to a supportive and creative community.

The Decision to Download

Resolved, Alex decided to take his first step. He navigated to the Blender website, where he was greeted by the slogan "Open Source 3D creation. Free to use for any purpose, forever." It was a welcoming call to beginners and professionals alike. With a click, the download began, and so did Alex's journey into the vast, uncharted waters of 3D artistry with Blender.

Anticipation of a New Beginning

As the download bar inched forward, Alex felt a mix of excitement and nervousness. He was about to embark on a journey that was both challenging and rewarding. He knew it wouldn't be easy, but he was ready to dive in and explore the potential of Blender, and more importantly, his own potential as a digital artist.

In this quiet corner of the library, a new chapter of Alex's creative life was about to begin. With Blender, he wasn't just downloading software; he was opening a door to endless possibilities of creation and imagination.

Commands from Chapter 1.

For Chapter 1, which covers Alex's initial exploration of Blender, the focus would be on basic navigation, understanding the interface, and simple object manipulation. Here are some key Blender commands and button combinations relevant to these early learning stages:

Basic Navigation

Rotate View: Hold the Middle Mouse Button and move the mouse.

Pan View: Hold Shift + Middle Mouse Button and move the mouse.

Zoom: Scroll the Middle Mouse Wheel, or hold Ctrl + Middle Mouse Button and move the mouse.

Interface and Layout

Switch Workspace: Click on the workspace tabs at the top or use Ctrl + Page Up/Page Down.

Toggle Sidebar: Press N to show/hide the sidebar in the 3D Viewport.

Toggle Properties Panel: Press Ctrl + T in the 3D Viewport.

Basic Object Manipulation

Add Object: Shift + A to open the Add menu, then choose the desired object (e.g., Mesh > Cube).

Select Object: Right-click on the object (left-click if you have selected left-click select).

Move Object: Select the object, then press G to grab and move it.

Rotate Object: Select the object, then press R to rotate.

Scale Object: Select the object, then press S to scale.

Basic Editing

Edit Mode: With an object selected, press Tab to toggle between Object Mode and Edit Mode.

Select Vertices, Edges, or Faces: In Edit Mode, use 1 (vertices), 2 (edges), or 3 (faces) on the number row.

Extrude: In Edit Mode, select a face or edge, then press E to extrude.

General Shortcuts

Undo: Ctrl + Z

Redo: Ctrl + Shift + Z

Save File: Ctrl + S

Render Preview: Press Z and select Rendered to view the scene in rendered mode.

These commands and shortcuts provide a foundation for beginners in Blender, as they cover the essential tasks Alex would encounter while starting his journey in 3D modeling and animation. Practicing these will help any beginner become more familiar and efficient with Blender's interface and basic functionalities.

Chapter 2: The Download Decision - Taking the Leap

After an afternoon of exploration and wonder, Alex found himself back in the solitude of his dorm room. The excitement from the library still lingered in his mind. He was on the cusp of a new venture, and the next step was clear: downloading Blender.

The Hurdle of Hesitation

As Alex opened his laptop, a flicker of hesitation crossed his mind. Questions swirled around: "Am I really ready for this? What if it's too complex?" But the memory of the vibrant Blender community, their encouraging words, and the stunning artworks he had seen, fueled his determination. This was not just about learning a software; it was about unlocking a new realm of creativity.

Finding the Right Source

He navigated to Blender's official website, a beacon for budding digital artists. The website was welcoming, informative, and straightforward. Here, Blender wasn't just presented as software, but as a journey of learning and creation. Alex noted the system requirements, ensuring his laptop met the necessary specifications.

Embracing the Open-Source Spirit

One aspect that stood out to Alex was Blender's open-source nature. It wasn't just free in terms of cost; it was a software built and continuously improved by a community of passionate users and developers. This collaborative spirit resonated with him, adding a layer of warmth to the technical world of 3D modeling.

The Moment of Commitment

Hovering over the download button, Alex took a deep breath. This was it. He clicked, and the download began. As the progress bar filled, so did his sense of anticipation. This small, yet significant act marked the beginning of what he hoped would be a long and fulfilling creative journey.

Preparation for the Odyssey

While the software downloaded, Alex decided to prepare himself further. He bookmarked tutorials, joined online forums, and even jotted down a list of projects he dreamed of creating. This was not just a waiting period; it was a time of building foundations for his future endeavors in Blender.

The Completion and the Onset

The download completed, a new icon gracing his desktop. For Alex, this was more than just a new application; it was a portal to a world where his ideas could take shape, where his creativity could find a new voice. With a mix of excitement and nervousness, he hovered over the icon, ready to embark on his Blender odyssey.

In the quiet of his room, with the night sky as his backdrop, Alex double-clicked the Blender icon. The program sprang to life, and with it, a new chapter of Alex's creative journey began.

Commands from Chapter 2.

In Chapter 2, which focuses on Alex's decision to download Blender and his initial setup, the relevant Blender commands and button combinations are related to installation, basic configuration, and familiarization with the software. Here's a guide to these initial steps:

Blender Installation and Setup

Downloading Blender: Visit the official Blender website (blender.org) and download the appropriate version for your operating system.

Installing Blender: Run the downloaded installer and follow the installation prompts.

Launching Blender: Open Blender from your applications or programs list.

Initial Configuration

Selecting Interaction Presets: Upon first launch, Blender may ask you to choose an interaction preset, such as 'Blender', '3ds Max', or 'Maya', which sets up your keymap and mouse selection preferences.

Adjusting Preferences: Access preferences by going to Edit > Preferences. Here, you can customize themes, add-ons, keymaps, and more.

Basic Orientation

Understanding Basic Layout: Familiarize yourself with the main areas - the 3D Viewport, Timeline, Outliner, and Properties Panel.

Viewport Navigation: Learn basic navigation controls - rotating (Middle Mouse Button), panning (Shift + Middle Mouse Button), and zooming (Scroll Wheel or Ctrl + Middle Mouse Button).

Object Mode vs. Edit Mode: Press Tab to switch between Object Mode (for object-level transformations) and Edit Mode (for detailed mesh editing).

First Actions in Blender

Adding and Deleting Objects: Shift + A to add objects, X or Delete to delete them.

Basic Object Manipulation: Use G (grab/move), R (rotate), and S (scale) for basic object transformations.

Saving Your Work: Press Ctrl + S to save your project.

Exploring Blender

Playing with Default Cube: Select the default cube and practice moving, rotating, and scaling it.

Render Preview: Press Z and select 'Rendered' to see a preview of what your scene looks like when rendered.

Accessing Blender Tutorials: Consider watching beginner tutorials from Blender's official YouTube channel or community creators.

These steps and commands are crucial for beginners like Alex, as they lay the groundwork for a comfortable and efficient start with Blender. They help in getting acquainted with the software, leading to a smoother learning curve as more complex features are explored later.

Chapter 3: First Launch - Entering a New World

The Blender icon on his desktop seemed to beckon Alex into a realm he had longed to explore. With a blend of excitement and a bit of nervousness, he clicked the icon. The software sprang to life, unveiling a world where his creative aspirations could take flight.

Embracing the Complexity

As Blender loaded, Alex was greeted with the default startup screen – a cube set against a grid, a simple beginning to complex possibilities. The interface was a tapestry of menus, toolbars, and panels, each promising a different path to creation. For a moment, Alex felt overwhelmed by the complexity, but he remembered the encouragement from the online forums: "Everyone starts with the cube."

The Cube: A Symbol of Beginning

He focused on the cube, the cornerstone of many Blender projects. It was more than a shape; it was a symbol of beginnings, a canvas waiting for his imagination. He played around, rotating and zooming in the 3D viewport, getting a feel for the navigation controls. Each movement brought a sense of achievement, a step further into the Blender universe.

Diving into Tutorials

Realizing the vastness of Blender's capabilities, Alex decided to follow some beginner tutorials. He found a series aimed at new users, perfect for understanding the basics. As he followed along, the interface started to become less intimidating, more like a map to guide him through this new terrain.

The Joy of Learning

Each tutorial was an adventure. He learned how to manipulate the default cube, transforming it through scaling, moving, and extruding. These were the building blocks of 3D modeling, and with each step, Alex's confidence grew. The cube began to evolve, taking on new shapes and forms under his command.

Experimentation and Exploration

With the basics under his belt, Alex began to experiment. He played with different geometric shapes, adding them to his scene, understanding how they could come together to form more complex structures. The thrill of creation was palpable, each click bringing a new discovery.

Overcoming Initial Challenges

The challenges were many. Sometimes, Alex found himself lost in the myriad of options, but he persevered, knowing that each hurdle was a learning opportunity. The Blender community was always there to help, with forums and videos that offered solutions and encouragement.

The End of the Beginning

As the clock ticked into the early hours of the morning, Alex leaned back in his chair, a sense of accomplishment washing over him. He had taken his first steps in Blender, ventured into a new world of digital art, and the journey had only just begun. The cube on his screen was no longer just a default object; it was a testament to his willingness to learn and grow.

In this quiet hour, Alex realized that his journey with Blender was more than learning software; it was about exploring the limits of his creativity and pushing beyond them. With each session, he was not just creating 3D models; he was shaping his future as a digital artist.

Commands from Chapter 3.

In Chapter 3, which is about Alex's first experience launching Blender and getting familiar with its primary features, the focus is on basic object manipulation, exploring the interface, and beginning to understand how Blender works. Here are some key Blender commands and button combinations relevant to this stage:

Basic Navigation and Interface

Orbit View: Hold the Middle Mouse Button and move the mouse.

Pan View: Hold Shift + Middle Mouse Button and move the mouse.

Zoom: Scroll the Middle Mouse Wheel, or hold Ctrl + Middle Mouse Button and move the mouse.

Toggle Sidebar (Toolshelf): Press T to show/hide the toolbar on the left side of the 3D Viewport.

Toggle Properties Panel: Press N to show/hide the properties region on the right side of the 3D Viewport.

Basic Object Manipulation

Add Object: Press Shift + A and select the desired object type (e.g., Mesh > Cube, Sphere, etc.).

Select Object: Right-click on an object (or left-click, depending on your selection preference).

Move Object: Select the object and press G to grab and move it.

Rotate Object: Select the object and press R to rotate it.

Scale Object: Select the object and press S to scale it.

Switching Between Object and Edit Modes

Switch Modes: Press Tab to toggle between Object Mode (for whole object manipulation) and Edit Mode (for detailed editing of mesh).

In Edit Mode

Select Vertices, Edges, or Faces: Press 1 for Vertex Select, 2 for Edge Select, and 3 for Face Select (in the number row, not Numpad).

Extrude: In Edit Mode, select a face, edge, or vertex, and press E to extrude.

Loop Cut: Press Ctrl + R and move the mouse to add loop cuts to your mesh.

Basic Viewing

View from Camera: Press Numpad 0 to view the scene from the camera's perspective.

Switch Between Perspective/Orthographic View: Press Numpad 5.

Rendering

Render Image: Press F12 to render your current scene.

View Rendered Image: Press F11 to toggle between the rendered image and the 3D Viewport.

General Shortcuts

Undo: Ctrl + Z

Redo: Ctrl + Shift + Z

Save File: Ctrl + S

These commands are fundamental for a beginner in Blender, like Alex, to get comfortable with the software's basic functionality, such as manipulating objects, navigating the interface, and performing simple modeling tasks.

Chapter 4: Navigating the Interface - Learning the Ropes

Alex, now more comfortable in his digital workspace, opened Blender with a newfound sense of confidence. Today, he was determined to understand the intricacies of the software's interface, a crucial step in mastering Blender.

The Layout: A Panoramic View

The Blender interface, at first glance, appeared as a complex array of panels and menus. Today, Alex decided to break it down, piece by piece. He started with the layout. There was the 3D Viewport, the heart of Blender where 3D models come to life. To the right, the Properties Panel, a control center for the details of his objects. The Timeline at the bottom awaited his venture into animation.

Customizing the Workspace

One of Blender's strengths, Alex learned, was its customization. He could tailor the interface to suit his workflow. As he experimented with dragging and resizing panels, he realized how Blender could adapt to his style, not the other way around. He set up a layout that felt intuitive, with easy access to the tools he used most.

Understanding the Tools

With the layout set, Alex delved into the tools. The Toolbar offered a selection of options for modeling, painting, sculpting, and more. He hovered over each tool, learning their names and functions. Select, Move, Rotate, Scale – these became his foundational tools, the basic verbs of his 3D grammar.

The Properties Panel - A Deep Dive

The Properties Panel was where the finer details lived. Here, Alex explored settings for rendering, object properties, material settings, and more. He realized this panel was like the backstage of his projects, where he could control the lighting, the textures, and the physics of his creations.

Shortcuts - The Blender's Secret

As he became more familiar with the interface, Alex discovered the power of shortcuts. Blender's use of keyboard shortcuts was extensive, enabling a faster, more efficient workflow. He started memorizing the most common ones, feeling like he was learning a new language – a language that made his creativity flow more freely.

Exploring the Editors

Blender offered a range of specialized editors for different tasks – the Node Editor for material and texture work, the UV/Image Editor for mapping textures, and more. Alex dabbled in each, getting a taste of the vast capabilities Blender offered. Each editor was a new world, and he was the explorer.

The Joy of Discovery

With each session, Alex felt more at home in Blender. The interface, once a maze of confusion, was now a map to guide his creativity. He found joy in the discovery, in understanding how each tool and panel could serve his artistic vision.

The End of the Day - A Reflective Pause

As the day wound down, Alex leaned back, a sense of satisfaction filling him. He had navigated the labyrinth of Blender's interface, and though there was still much to learn, he felt ready. Ready to create, to experiment, and to bring his ideas to life in this digital canvas.

In the soft glow of his computer screen, Alex realized that Blender was more than software; it was a medium of expression, and he was just beginning to paint his first strokes.

Commands from Chapter 4.

In Chapter 4, focusing on Alex's further exploration of Blender's interface and features, we'll cover more advanced aspects like customizing the workspace, using different tools, and understanding the Properties Panel. Here are relevant Blender commands and button combinations for these tasks:

Customizing the Workspace

Change Workspace Layout: Click on the layout tabs at the top of the Blender window or use Ctrl + Page Up/Page Down.

Split and Join Areas: Right-click on a border between two areas to split or join them.

Toggle Fullscreen Area: Hover over an area and press Ctrl + Space to toggle fullscreen mode for that area.

Exploring Tools in the Toolbar

Access Tools: Press T to open the Toolbar on the left side of the 3D Viewport.

Select Tool: Click on a tool icon or use corresponding hotkeys (displayed next to the tool names).

Tool Settings: Adjust settings for each tool in the panel below the Toolbar.

Using the Properties Panel

Access Properties Panel: Press N to open the panel on the right side of the 3D Viewport.

Explore Different Tabs: Click on different tabs like Render, Object, Modifier, Material, etc., to access various settings.

Adjust Object Properties: Select an object and use the Object tab to change its properties like location, rotation, scale, etc.

Working with Different Editors

Switch Editors: Click on the editor type menu (in the corner of each window) to switch between editors like 3D Viewport, UV/Image Editor, Node Editor, etc.

Use Timeline for Basic Animation: At the bottom, use the Timeline editor to play animations, set keyframes, etc.

Using Shortcuts for Efficiency

Common Object Manipulation Shortcuts: G (grab/move), R (rotate), S (scale), E (extrude), F (make face/edge).

Quick Snapping Options: Press Shift + Tab to toggle snapping, use Ctrl while transforming to temporarily enable snapping.

Hide/Reveal Objects: Press H to hide selected objects, Alt + H to reveal all hidden objects.

General Shortcuts and Tips

Search for Functions: Press F3 to search for and execute Blender functions.

Undo/Redo: Ctrl + Z for undo, Ctrl + Shift + Z for redo.

Saving Work: Ctrl + S to save your Blender file.

Viewport Shading Modes: Press Z and choose a shading mode (Wireframe, Solid, Material Preview, Rendered).

These commands and shortcuts are essential for navigating Blender's interface more efficiently and exploring its various features, which would be particularly relevant for someone like Alex as he becomes more familiar with Blender's capabilities.

Chapter 5: Your First Project - Creating a Simple Object

With a newfound understanding of Blender's interface, Alex was ready to embark on his first real project. Today, he would create something from scratch, a simple object, but his own creation nonetheless.

Choosing the Project

Alex pondered what his first project should be. He wanted something achievable yet challenging enough to apply what he had learned. After some thought, he decided on a classic choice for beginners: modeling a simple coffee mug. It was a perfect project to practice basic modeling and texturing skills.

Setting the Foundation

He started by deleting the default cube and adding a cylinder, the base shape for his mug. Using the skills he had learned from the tutorials, he adjusted the cylinder's dimensions, setting the foundation for his mug. Each action was deliberate, a dance between his vision and the software's capabilities.

Sculpting the Mug

With the basic shape in place, Alex began to sculpt the mug. He extruded the top edge to create the lip of the mug and adjusted the vertices to get the perfect curvature. The process was meditative, and he found himself lost in the flow of creation.

Crafting the Handle

Next came the handle – a crucial part of any mug. Alex used a torus shape as a starting point and modified it to fit the side of the mug. It was a tricky process, requiring careful manipulation of the mesh, but Alex was up for the challenge. When he finally attached the handle to the mug, a sense of accomplishment washed over him.

Adding Color and Texture

With the modeling complete, it was time to add color and texture. Alex decided on a simple ceramic texture and a glossy finish. He experimented with Blender's material properties, adjusting the color, specularity, and roughness until he was satisfied with the look.

The Final Touches

As a final touch, Alex decided to add a simple scene – a table for the mug to sit on, and a light source to give the scene depth. He played with the lighting settings, watching as the shadows and highlights interacted with the mug's surface, giving it a sense of realism.

Rendering the Scene

With everything in place, it was time to render the scene. Alex hit the render button, and Blender began its magic. As the image slowly came to life on the screen, Alex's heart raced. This was the moment of truth.

The Reward of Creation

The render completed, and there it was – Alex's first Blender project, a simple yet beautiful coffee mug. It wasn't perfect, but it was his creation, a tangible result of his efforts and learning. He sat back, a smile spreading across his face, already thinking of what he could create next.

In this first project, Alex had not just made a 3D object; he had crossed a threshold. He was no longer just a beginner; he was a creator, ready to dive deeper into the endless possibilities Blender offered.

Commands from Chapter 5.

In Chapter 5, Alex embarks on his first modeling project in Blender. This stage involves creating and modifying basic shapes, adding textures, and setting up a simple scene. Here are Blender commands and button combinations that are especially useful for these tasks:

Basic Modeling

Add Object: Shift + A to open the Add menu, then choose a shape (e.g., Mesh > Cylinder for the mug body)

Select Object: Right-click on an object (or left-click if you have left-click select enabled).

Move, Rotate, Scale: Use G to grab/move, R to rotate, S to scale the object.

Edit Mode: Press Tab to switch to Edit Mode for detailed editing of the mesh.

Extrude: In Edit Mode, select a face or edge and press E to extrude.

Loop Cut: Press Ctrl + R then move the mouse to add loop cuts.

Texturing and Materials

Open Material Properties: In the Properties Panel, go to the Material tab.

Add New Material: Click 'New' to add a new material to the selected object.

Adjust Material Settings: Modify properties like Base Color, Specularity, Roughness, etc.

UV Unwrapping for Textures: In Edit Mode, select all faces (A), then U to unwrap. Adjust the unwrap in the UV/Image Editor.

Setting Up a Simple Scene

Add a Plane for the Table: Shift + A > Mesh > Plane. Scale it to resemble a table surface.

Set Camera View: Add a camera (Shift + A > Camera) and position it with G and R. Press Numpad 0 to see through the camera.

Basic Lighting: Add a light source (Shift + A > Light) and adjust its position and settings.

Rendering the Scene

Switch to Camera View: Press Numpad 0.

Render the Image: Press F12.

Adjust Render Settings: In the Properties Panel, under the Render tab, adjust settings like resolution and samples.

General Shortcuts

Undo/Redo: Ctrl + Z for undo, Ctrl + Shift + Z for redo.

Save File: Ctrl + S.

View Shading Modes: Press Z and select a mode (e.g., Wireframe, Solid, Rendered).

These commands and shortcuts are integral to the process of creating a basic 3D model like a coffee mug, applying materials and textures, setting up a simple scene with lighting, and rendering the final image in Blender. They provide a solid foundation for any beginner working on their first project.

Chapter 6: Sculpting and Texturing - Bringing Shapes to Life

Buoyed by the success of his first project, Alex was eager to delve deeper into Blender. His next venture was to explore the realms of sculpting and texturing, crucial skills for bringing his 3D models to life.

The World of Digital Sculpting

Alex started his new journey by choosing a subject for sculpting. He decided on something organic and challenging - a human face. The complexity of human features would be a significant step up from his coffee mug, but he felt ready for the challenge.

Setting the Stage

He began by creating a basic mesh of a head. Using reference images, he meticulously shaped the outline, ensuring the proportions were accurate. This initial step was crucial; a well-defined base mesh set the foundation for detailed sculpting.

Sculpting Details

With the base ready, Alex dove into sculpting. Blender's sculpting tools were like digital chisels and brushes, allowing him to mold his mesh into a lifelike face. He worked on the details - the curve of the cheek, the ridge of the eyebrows, the contours of the lips. The process was intricate and required patience, but Alex was absorbed in the creation.

Discovering Texturing

Once satisfied with the sculpting, Alex turned to texturing. He learned about Blender's texturing capabilities which would allow him to add skin tones, fine lines, and subtle imperfections to his model. Texturing was not just coloring; it was about giving the model a skin, a sense of realism.

Applying Textures

He experimented with various textures, adjusting parameters to see how they affected the model. It was a process of trial and error, but with each attempt, he learned more about how textures interacted with light and shadow, giving depth and realism to his creation.

The Challenge of Realism

Texturing a human face was challenging. Alex had to consider the subtleties of human skin - its variations in color, its texture, and how it reacted to light. He spent hours tweaking settings, determined to get as close to realism as he could.

Rendering the Sculpted Model

Finally, it was time to render his sculpted and textured model. Alex adjusted the lighting to highlight the details of the face, then hit render. As the image materialized, he watched in awe. The face, with its detailed textures and lifelike appearance, was a testament to his hard work and learning.

Reflections on Growth

As Alex looked at his finished model, he felt a sense of pride. He had come a long way from his simple coffee mug. Sculpting and texturing had opened up a new world of possibilities in Blender, and he was just scratching the surface.

In that moment, Alex realized that each project was a stepping stone, not just in learning Blender, but in understanding the art of 3D modeling. With each new skill, he was not only creating digital art; he was sculpting his path as an artist.

Commands from Chapter 6.

In Chapter 6, Alex dives into sculpting and texturing in Blender, which involves more specialized commands and techniques. Here are the key Blender commands and button combinations relevant to sculpting and texturing:

Sculpting in Blender

Switch to Sculpt Mode: Select your object, then go to the mode selection menu and choose 'Sculpt Mode'.

Choose a Sculpting Brush: Use the toolbar to select different sculpting brushes like Grab, Clay, Smooth, etc.

Adjust Brush Size and Strength: Press F to adjust the brush size, Shift + F to adjust brush strength.

Dynamic Topology (Dyntopo): In the Sculpt Mode properties, enable 'Dyntopo' for dynamic mesh tessellation.

Basic Texturing

Open UV/Image Editor: Switch one of your workspaces to 'UV/Image Editor' for UV mapping.

Unwrap Mesh: In Edit Mode, select all faces (A), then press U to unwrap. This projects your 3D mesh to a 2D layout for texturing.

Create New Material: In the Properties Panel, go to the Material tab and click 'New'.

Apply Texture: In the Material's settings, under the 'Base Color', click the dot icon to add a texture (e.g., Image Texture) and open your image file.

Advanced Texturing - Nodes

Switch to Shader Editor: Change your workspace to 'Shader Editor' for advanced texturing using nodes.

Add Texture Nodes: Press Shift + A in Shader Editor to add nodes. Typically, you'll add an 'Image Texture' node connected to the 'Base Color' of the 'Principled BSDF' shader.

Connect Nodes: Drag to connect nodes. For instance, connect the 'Color' output of the Image Texture node to the 'Base Color' input of the Principled BSDF shader.

Rendering Your Sculpted and Textured Model

Set Up Lighting and Camera: Ensure your scene has appropriate lighting and the camera is positioned correctly.

Switch Render Engine to Cycles for Realism (Optional): In the Render settings, switch the engine from 'Eevee' to 'Cycles' for more realistic rendering.

Render the Scene: Press F12 to render the image.

General Shortcuts and Tips

Smooth Brush: Hold Shift while sculpting to smooth areas.

Masking: Ctrl + left-click to paint a mask in Sculpt Mode.

Symmetry: In Sculpt Mode, use the symmetry options to mirror your sculpting actions.

Save Frequently: Ctrl + S to save your work.

These commands and techniques are essential for a Blender user venturing into the world of sculpting and texturing, allowing them to create more detailed and realistic 3D models.

Chapter 7: Lighting and Rendering - The Art of Visualization

After mastering the fundamentals of modeling and texturing, Alex was ready to tackle the next crucial aspect of 3D art in Blender: lighting and rendering. This stage would breathe life into his creations, transforming them from mere models into vivid, realistic scenes.

Understanding Lighting

Alex began by exploring the different types of lights available in Blender. He learned about point lights, spotlights, area lights, and the sun lamp. Each had its unique properties and uses. He experimented with these lights, observing how they affected the mood and atmosphere of his scene.

The Magic of Shadows

He quickly realized the importance of shadows in adding depth and realism. By adjusting the light's strength, color, and position, he could create a range of effects - from soft, subtle shadows to sharp, dramatic contrasts. The right lighting could tell a story on its own.

Exploring Rendering Engines

Next, Alex delved into Blender's rendering engines - Eevee and Cycles. Eevee was a real-time engine, great for quick previews and animations, while Cycles offered photorealistic rendering. He tried both, marveling at how each engine brought his models to life in different ways.

The Cycles Experiment

Drawn to the realism of Cycles, Alex decided to render his human face model using this engine. He set up the scene, adjusted the lighting, and hit render. The process was slower than Eevee, but as the image gradually appeared on the screen, Alex was amazed. The details, the textures, the play of light and shadow - it was like seeing his model for the first time.

Fine-Tuning the Scene

With the initial render complete, Alex began fine-tuning. He adjusted the lighting angles, changed the background, and experimented with different camera settings. Each render brought new insights, and with every tweak, the scene moved closer to the vision in his mind.

Discovering Compositing

Alex also discovered the power of compositing in Blender. This post-processing stage allowed him to adjust colors, add effects, and refine the final image. It was like the final coat of paint on a masterpiece.

The Final Render

Finally, satisfied with his adjustments, Alex rendered the scene one last time. This final render was everything he had hoped for - the model looked lifelike, bathed in just the right amount of light, with shadows falling perfectly.

Reflecting on the Journey

As he looked at his finished piece, Alex felt a surge of pride. He had not only created a 3D model but had brought it to life with lighting and rendering. It was a testament to his journey in Blender - from a novice to an artist capable of creating scenes that told stories.

In that moment, Alex realized that Blender was more than software; it was a medium through which he could express his creativity, transforming the visions in his mind into visual realities.

Commands from Chapter 7.

Lighting

Add a Light: Shift + A to open the Add menu, then navigate to Light and choose the type (e.g., Point, Sun, Spot, Area).

Move Light: Select the light, then press G to grab and move it. Use X, Y, or Z to constrain movement to an axis.

Scale Light Size/Radius: Select the light, then press S and move the mouse to scale.

Adjust Light Properties: With the light selected, properties like strength, color, and shadows can be adjusted in the Properties Panel under the Light tab.

Rendering with Cycles

Switch to Cycles Render Engine: In the Properties Panel, go to the Render tab and select Cycles from the drop-down menu at the top.

Render Image: Press F12 to render the current frame.

View Rendered Image: Press F11 to view the last rendered image.

Adjust Render Settings: In the Properties Panel, under the Render tab, you can adjust various settings like resolution, sampling, and output format.

Camera Setup

Add Camera: Shift + A, navigate to Camera.

Position Camera: Select the camera, then press G to move, and R to rotate. Use G + Middle Mouse Button to zoom in/out.

Camera View: With the camera selected, press Numpad 0 to view the scene from the camera's perspective.

Compositing (Post-Processing)

Open Compositor: Switch to the Compositing workspace from the top menu.

Enable Use Nodes: In the Compositor, make sure Use Nodes is checked.

Add Nodes: Shift + A to add nodes. Common nodes for post-processing include Color Balance, Brightness/Contrast, and Blur.

General Shortcuts

Undo: Ctrl + Z

Redo: Ctrl + Shift + Z

Save File: Ctrl + S

These commands will assist in performing basic tasks related to lighting, rendering, and setting up a scene in Blender, as Alex would have done in the chapter. Remember, practicing these commands will help in developing a smoother workflow in Blender.

Chapter 8: Animation Basics - Giving Motion to Models

After mastering sculpting and texturing, Alex's next adventure in Blender was to breathe life into his creations through animation. He was about to step into the captivating world of moving art.

Understanding Keyframes

Alex started with the basics of animation: keyframes. These are the pillars of animation, marking the start and end points of any motion. He learned to insert a keyframe by pressing I and selecting the type of keyframe, like 'Location', 'Rotation', or 'Scale'.

Animating the Simple Mug

As a practice exercise, Alex decided to animate his coffee mug. He wanted to make it rotate. He placed his first keyframe at the beginning of the timeline, rotated the mug 360 degrees along the Z-axis, and inserted another keyframe at the end of the timeline.

The Timeline and Dope Sheet

The timeline at the bottom of the screen became his control panel. Here, he could scrub through the animation, watch the mug rotate, and adjust the keyframes as needed. The Dope Sheet, an extended version of the timeline, provided him with a more detailed view of all keyframes and their timing.

Adding Easing and Interpolation

Alex learned about the concepts of easing and interpolation. These techniques make animations more natural by controlling the acceleration and deceleration of motion. In the Graph Editor, he adjusted the Bezier' handles to smooth out the movement of the mug.

Exploring Simple Character Animation

Eager to try something more complex, Alex decided to animate a basic human figure. He started by rigging the model with a simple armature, then posing the character in various keyframes to create a basic walk cycle.

Understanding Rigging

Rigging was a new challenge. Alex had to create a skeleton for his character and then 'skin' the mesh, so it deformed naturally with the skeleton. He learned about bones, weight painting, and parent-child relationships between the bones and the mesh.

Creating a Walk Cycle

With the rigging complete, Alex moved on to animating a walk cycle. He studied the human gait, breaking it down into key poses: the contact position, the down position, the passing position, and the up position. Frame by frame, he brought his character to life.

Rendering the Animation

Once satisfied with the walk cycle, Alex rendered the animation. He adjusted the frame rate and the output settings, then hit 'Render Animation'. Watching the character walk across the screen was a magical moment. It was no longer just a model; it was a character with motion, a story to tell.

Reflections on Learning Animation

As Alex finished his day, he realized how far he had come. Animation was not just about moving objects; it was about creating an illusion of life. Each keyframe was a breath, each motion a heartbeat. He had unlocked a new dimension of creativity in Blender, a world where his models could move and interact.

In this new realm of animation, Alex saw endless possibilities - stories to be told, characters to be brought t life, and worlds to be created. He was no longer just a 3D artist; he was becoming a storyteller.

Commands from Chapter 8.

For Chapter 8, focusing on Alex's introduction to basic animation in Blender, here are the key commands and button combinations he would use for tasks related to keyframing, rigging, and animating:

Basic Keyframe Animation

Insert Keyframe: Select the object, move to the desired frame on the timeline, make your transformation (move, rotate, scale), then press I and choose the type of keyframe (e.g., Location, Rotation, Scale).

Timeline Navigation: Use the timeline at the bottom to scrub through the animation. Right Arrow and Left Arrow keys to step frame by frame.

Play Animation: Press Spacebar to play/pause the animation.

Dope Sheet and Graph Editor

Open Dope Sheet: Change one of the windows to 'Dope Sheet' for a detailed view of keyframes.

Adjust Keyframes in Dope Sheet: Move, scale, or duplicate keyframes in the Dope Sheet.

Open Graph Editor: Switch to the Graph Editor to adjust interpolation and easing of keyframes.

Rigging and Armature

Add Armature: Shift + A and select 'Armature' to add bones.

Edit Bones: In Edit Mode (Tab), select and manipulate bones to fit your character's mesh.

Parent Mesh to Armature: Select the mesh, then the armature, press Ctrl + P and choose 'With Automatic Weights' for automatic skinning.

Basic Walk Cycle

Pose Mode for Armature: Select the armature and press Ctrl + Tab to switch to Pose Mode for posing the skeleton.

Insert Keyframes for Poses: Position the bones for a pose, then insert keyframes for the required bone transformations.

Rendering Animation

Set Frame Range: In the Properties Panel, under the Render tab, set the 'Start' and 'End' frame for your animation.

Set Output Format: In the same tab, under Output, choose your file format for the rendered animation (e.g., AVI, MPEG).

Render Animation: Press Ctrl + F12 to start rendering the animation.

General Shortcuts

Undo/Redo: Ctrl + Z for undo, Ctrl + Shift + Z for redo.

Save File: Ctrl + S.

These commands are crucial for a beginner in Blender to start experimenting with animation, covering everything from setting basic keyframes to creating a simple walk cycle and rendering the animation.

Chapter 9: Exploring Advanced Features - Beyond the Basics

Having gained confidence in modeling, texturing, and basic animation, Alex was now ready to explore Blender's more advanced features. This chapter marks his journey into the realms of particle systems, physics simulations, and complex animation techniques.

Delving into Particle Systems

Alex's first venture was into particle systems, a powerful feature for creating effects like rain, smoke, or even hair. He started by adding a particle system to a simple sphere, turning it into a fizzy, bubbling object. Experimenting with different settings, he learned how to control the number, size, and behavior of the particles.

Physics and Cloth Simulation

Next, Alex dived into physics simulations. He created a flag and used Blender's Cloth Simulation to make it ripple realistically in the wind. Adjusting parameters like wind strength and cloth stiffness, he marveled at the lifelike movements he could create, all within the digital world of Blender.

Advanced Animation with NLA Editor

With a solid grasp of basic keyframe animation, Alex now explored the Non-Linear Animation (NLA) Editor. This tool allowed him to mix and blend different animations together. He created a simple character and made it walk, wave, and jump, then used the NLA Editor to seamlessly blend these actions into a continuous, complex animation.

Rigging and Weight Painting

Taking his rigging skills further, Alex learned about weight painting. This technique fine-tunes how the mesh moves with the armature. Painting different weights on the mesh, he ensured that his character's joints bent naturally, with muscles flexing and skin stretching realistically.

Exploring Node-Based Materials

In his journey with texturing, Alex now delved deeper into Blender's node-based material system. He created complex materials by combining different nodes, like texture, shader, and math nodes. This allowed him to create more realistic and intricate textures, like rusted metal or wet ground.

Compositing for Post-Production

Alex's next step was compositing, Blender's powerful tool for post-production. He combined different rendered layers and added effects like blurs, color grading, and glows. This process gave his final renders a polished, professional look.

Challenges and Discoveries

Each new feature presented its own set of challenges, but Alex was undeterred. With each hurdle, he gained new skills and a deeper understanding of Blender's capabilities. He frequented forums and tutorials, constantly learning from the vast community of Blender users.

Reflections on Advanced 3D Artistry

As he wrapped up his day, Alex looked back at his journey with Blender. Starting from simple models and basic animations, he had progressed to creating complex scenes with realistic physics, intricate materials, and advanced animation techniques. His journey was a testament to his dedication and Blender's limitless potential.

In exploring these advanced features, Alex had not just learned new tools; he had expanded his creative horizon. He was now not just a user of Blender, but an artist capable of bringing his most complex visions to life.

Commands from Chapter 9.

In Chapter 9, focusing on advanced features in Blender, Alex would use a variety of commands and shortcuts for tasks like handling particle systems, cloth simulation, advanced animation, and node-based materials. Here are some of those key commands and button combinations:

Particle Systems

Add Particle System: Select the object, go to the Particle Properties tab in the Properties Panel, and click 'New' to add a particle system.

Adjust Particle Settings: In the Particle Properties tab, modify settings like number of particles, emission rate, lifetime, physics, etc.

Particle Edit Mode: To edit particles like hair, switch to 'Particle Edit' mode from the mode menu.

Cloth Simulation

Add Cloth Modifier: Select the object (e.g., a flag), go to the Modifier Properties tab, and add a 'Cloth' modifier.

Adjust Cloth Settings: Modify properties like stiffness, damping, and collision in the Cloth modifier.

Bake Simulation: In the Physics Properties tab, under the Cloth settings, use 'Bake' to calculate and save the cloth movement.

Advanced Animation with NLA Editor

Access NLA Editor: Change one of your Blender windows to the NLA Editor.

Add Action to NLA Track: In the NLA Editor, add your keyframed actions to the NLA tracks for mixing and blending.

Tweak Mode: Enter Tweak Mode to make adjustments to individual actions within the NLA Editor.

Rigging and Weight Painting

Add Armature for Rigging: Shift + A > Armature.

Weight Painting Mode: With the mesh selected, switch to 'Weight Paint' mode to paint influence weights for the bones.

Assign Automatic Weights: Select mesh, then armature, press Ctrl + P and choose 'With Automatic Weights

Node-Based Materials

Access Shader Editor: Change the workspace to 'Shader Editor' for node-based material editing.

Add Nodes: Shift + A in the Shader Editor to add texture nodes, shader nodes, etc.

Connect Nodes: Drag to connect nodes' sockets (e.g., connect a texture node to a shader node).

Compositing

Switch to Compositing Workspace: Use the compositing workspace or change a window to the 'Compositor'.

Enable Use Nodes: In the Compositor, check 'Use Nodes'.

Add and Connect Nodes: Shift + A to add compositing nodes and drag to connect them for post-processing effects.

General Tips and Shortcuts

Bake Physics Simulations: For simulations, use 'Bake' in physics tabs to calculate and save physics movements.

Camera View: Numpad 0 to toggle camera view.

Render Animation: Ctrl + F12.

These commands cover a range of advanced functionalities in Blender, enabling Alex to create complex scenes with dynamic elements, sophisticated materials, and refined post-production effects.

Chapter 10: Completing Your First Project - From Start to Finish

As Alex's journey with Blender reached a crescendo, he embarked on his most ambitious project yet: a short animated film that would encapsulate all the skills he had learned. This chapter is about bringing together modeling, texturing, lighting, animation, and post-production into one cohesive project.

Conceptualizing the Project

Alex began by sketching out his ideas. He decided on a narrative - a simple story about a day in the life of a robot in a futuristic city. This concept would allow him to showcase his skills in character design, environmental modeling, and storytelling through animation.

Building the World

He started with the environment, creating the buildings, streets, and props that made up his futuristic city. He applied his knowledge of modeling and texturing to give each element a distinct futuristic yet believable look. The city slowly came to life, block by block, in Blender's 3D viewport.

Designing the Characters

Next, Alex focused on his main character, the robot. He wanted it to have a unique personality. He meticulously modeled the robot, ensuring each joint and limb had the right proportions and mechanics. He then rigged and weight-painted the model for animation.

Texturing and Materials

Alex spent time on texturing, using Blender's node-based system to create materials that looked realistic. He gave attention to details like metal wear-and-tear, glass reflections, and the play of light on different surfaces.

Animating the Story

With the scene and characters set, Alex moved on to animation. He plotted out the robot's movement through the city, from waking up in the morning to wandering the neon-lit streets at night. He used keyframe animation and the NLA editor to bring smooth and lifelike motion to the character.

Adding Lighting and Rendering

Alex set up the lighting to match different times of the day, creating mood and atmosphere. He used Blender's Cycles renderer to bring out the realism in his scenes, carefully setting up camera angles and compositions for each shot.

Post-Production and Compositing

In the final stage, Alex used Blender's compositing tools for post-production. He added visual effects like glows and lens flares, color graded the scenes for visual appeal, and edited the rendered shots into a seamless short film.

The Final Product

After days of rendering, Alex's project was complete. He sat back and watched his film - a story told entirely through the lens of Blender. It was a testament to his journey, from a novice to a skilled Blender artist.

Reflections and Future Aspirations

As the credits rolled in his short film, Alex felt a profound sense of accomplishment. He had traversed the vast landscape of Blender's capabilities, from simple models to a complete animated film. He was already brimming with ideas for his next project, each more ambitious than the last.

In Blender, Alex had found more than just a software; he had discovered a medium through which to express his creativity, a tool that turned his imagination into visual stories. His journey was a reminder that with passion, dedication, and the right tools, one can bring any dream to life.

Commands from Chapter 10.

In the final chapter, where Alex completes a comprehensive project in Blender, he integrates various skills and techniques. Here are some key Blender commands and button combinations for tasks he would undertake in this comprehensive project:

Environmental Modeling

Add Objects for Environment: Shift + A to add meshes for buildings, streets, etc.

Duplicate Objects: Shift + D to duplicate items like street lamps or buildings.

Object Modifiers for Details: Use modifiers (e.g., Array, Bevel) for repetitive structures or smooth edges.

Character Design and Rigging

Create Armature for Character: Shift + A, then select Armature for the robot.

Rigging and Skinning: Ctrl + P and select 'With Automatic Weights' for parenting the mesh to the armature with weight painting.

Pose Character: In Pose Mode (Ctrl + Tab), pose the character for keyframes.

Texturing and Materials

Open Shader Editor: Change workspace to Shader Editor for advanced material creation.

Node-Based Material Creation: Shift + A in Shader Editor to add and connect nodes like Textures, BSDFs, etc

UV Unwrapping for Textures: In Edit Mode, select all (A), then U for unwrapping mesh.

Animation and Keyframing

Insert Keyframes: Select object/bone, move to the desired frame, make transformation, then I and choose keyframe type.

Timeline and Dope Sheet for Animation: Use the timeline for overall animation control and Dope Sheet for detailed keyframe management.

Graph Editor for Refinement: Use the Graph Editor for adjusting interpolation and easing of keyframes.

Lighting and Rendering

Set Up Lights: Shift + A to add lights; adjust properties in the Light tab.

Camera Positioning: Numpad 0 for camera view; position camera with G and R.

Render Settings: In the Properties Panel, under the Render tab, adjust settings like output resolution, sampling, and file format.

Render Image/Animation: F12 for image rendering, Ctrl + F12 for animation rendering.

Compositing and Post-Production

Switch to Compositing Workspace: Use Blender's compositing workspace for post-processing.

Use Nodes in Compositor: Shift + A to add nodes like Color Correction, Blur, Glare.

Render Layers and Passes: Use render layers and passes for complex compositing.

Final Editing

Open Video Sequence Editor: Compile and edit rendered scenes into a final video.

Add Video Strips: Import rendered scenes/clips into the Video Sequence Editor.

Adjust Sequences: Cut, move, and overlap strips as needed for final editing.

General Shortcuts

Save File: Ctrl + S.

Undo/Redo: Ctrl + Z / Ctrl + Shift + Z.

Quick Switch between Modes: Tab for Edit Mode, Ctrl + Tab for Pose Mode.

These commands and shortcuts are integral for Alex to complete a comprehensive project in Blender, bringing together various aspects like environmental modeling, character animation, texturing, lighting, and post-production to create a cohesive animated film.